The Anchor of Our Purest Thoughts (Book 6)

TRAPPED BY ASSUMPTIONS

How to Break Mental Traps and Keep Your Mind Sharp

DR. CHONG CHEN

Brain & Life Publishing
London

Copyright © 2018 by Chong Chen, PhD

All Rights Reserved. No reproduction of any part of this book may take place without the written permission of the publisher, except in the case of brief quotations embodied in book reviews and other educational and research uses permitted by copyright law.

ISBN 9781912533077 Paperback

Brain & Life Publishing

27 Old Gloucester Street, London, U.K.

First Printing, November 2018

For information about special needs for bulk purchases, sales promotions, and educational needs, please contact orders@brainandlife.net.

The Anchor of Our Purest Thoughts Series

1. *Fitness Powered Brains: Optimize Your Productivity, Leadership and Performance*

2. *Chocolate and the Nobel Prize: The Book of Brain Food*

3. *Cleverland: The Science of How Nature Nurtures*

4. *The Tale of Two Minds: The Art and Science of Decision-making in Everyday Life*

5. *Strategic Memory: The Natural History of Learning and Forgetting*

6. *Trapped by Assumptions: How to Break Mental Traps and Keep Your Mind Sharp*

To Arisa and my parents for their love and support

Table of Contents

Introduction 1

Assumption 1. Confirmed Ideas Are Solid and True ... 3

    Christopher Columbus's Confirmation Trips 5

    The Confirmation Strategy We Use and Why to Reject and Falsify It 9

    The Hypothetico-Deductive Method for Reasoning 13

    Confirmation Biases in Psychologists 15

    Confirmation Biases in Medical Doctors 18

    Confirmation Biases in Our Everyday Lives 21

    Avoiding Confirmation Bias 26

Assumption 2. "Handsome Soldiers Are Good at Shooting" 27

    The Halo Effect 28

    Too High an Expectation Causes Disappointment 32

    The Illusion of Business: Cisco's Story 34

    Risks and Benefits Under the Halo Effect 37

    Overcoming the Halo Effect 43

Assumption 3. Fluent Memories Are More Compelling and Trustable 46

    "If I Cannot Recall It, It's Perhaps Not That True/Important…" 46

Sampling Traps 50

What Happens after a Man Views an Ad 20 Times? ... 52

The Mere Exposure Effect 54

Human Kindness, or Thinking Bias? 57

Be Careful What You Expose Yourself to 61

Assumption 4. Being Simple and Salient Is Being Real and Special 63

"Fluent" Stocks Make More Money 63

Easy-to-read Documents Are More Real and Trustworthy 66

A Picture Is Worth a Thousand Words 68

Vivid Details Are More Trustworthy 70

Be Careful What You Imagine 73

Convince Yourself with Imaginations: The Planning Fallacy 75

Look at the Evidence, Objectively 77

References 79

Index 87

About the Author 89

Introduction

It's natural to make assumptions. Often, we have incomplete information about a situation and in trying to make sense of the situation, we can't help but fill in the blanks ourselves. Consequently, we fill in the blanks with our INTERPRETATION of the situation.

Our interpretations, however, turn out to be full of assumptions. Usually they are beliefs we previously learned, which we often take for granted and accept unquestioningly. Therefore, we make assumptions often without realizing it.

Based on these assumptions, we make inferences and in many cases, they help us deal with the situation and navigate the sophisticated world.

However, some assumptions are not only incorrect, but also dangerous. Some of them arise due to the nature of the human mind and the characteristics of how our brain processes information. Some arise because we have always used them and they seemed to work quite well. But if we dissect them seriously and in an objective way, we'll find that many assumptions are baseless and lead us to conclusions that are wrong and have serious consequences.

In this book, I'll lay out four common assumptions and show you how they misguide us in everyday life.

Since I realized the "logic" behind these assumptions was flawed and stopped believing them, I started to notice things that have been always out there, but escaped me due to my wishful assumptions. Discarding these assumptions gave me a new pair of eyes.

Instead of making assumptions, I do my best to collect information and statistics. I try to see the big picture. Thanks to that, I'm now much more relieved and freer to think in an objective way. I'm sure it will help you too. Good luck!

Assumption 1. Confirmed Ideas Are Solid and True

Anyone looking for confirmation will find enough of it to deceive himself—and no doubt his peers.

—Nassim Nicholas Taleb, The Black Swan: The Impact of the Highly Improbable (2007)

Figure 1-1 Portrait of Christopher Columbus

The Italian navigator Christopher Columbus loved sailing and adventures since his childhood. After reading *The Travels of Marco Polo*, he looked forward to the fertile Asia and was eager to sail to China and India. After years of lobbying, he finally persuaded the Spanish royal family to fund him in order to open up the sea route to the Eastern World. In 1492, Columbus successfully crossed the Atlantic Ocean and arrived in the New World.

The American historian George E. Nunn believed Columbus actually had three major discoveries: (1) the New World, (2) the best sea route westwards from Europe to North America, and (3) the best sea route eastward from North America back to Europe.

The New World concealed Columbus's other two discoveries, but it was the latter two that opened up the doors for European explorers to colonize the New World in the coming centuries. It was also the latter two discoveries that helped European scientists and naturalists travel to the Americas for scientific investigations and explorations. Charles Darwin, who joined the British Navy survey ship, *HMS Beagle*, in 1831, Alfred Wallace, who joined *HMS Mischief* in 1848, and a dozen other famous naturalists should all thank Columbus.

However, despite such a great contribution, things did not go well with Columbus after his discoveries. On the issue of where the New World was, Columbus seemed to have become a "slave of dreams". He firmly believed he had arrived in Asia and was determined to search everywhere for evidence that confirmed his belief.

Assumption 1. Confirmed Ideas Are Solid and True

Christopher Columbus's Confirmation Trips

A shrub that smelled like cinnamon was seen by Columbus as a valuable oriental spice. An aroma of Latin America's local olive plant was considered the Asian variant of the Mediterranean Mastic Pine. An unknown inedible nut was believed to be the coconut described by Marco Polo. The tree roots dug up by the crew were but ordinary rhubarb; Columbus thought they were rare, Chinese medicinal rhubarbs. Although he never found "Great Khan" and "the Island of Endless Gold", Columbus still believed the indirect evidence above could prove he had arrived in the East.

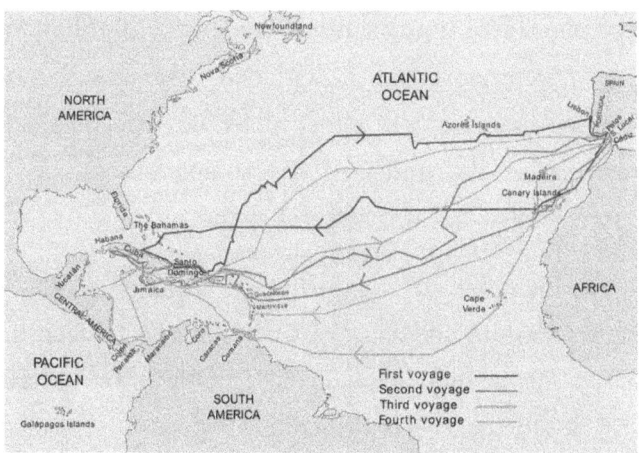

Figure 1-2 The Voyages of Christopher Columbus.
Source:
https://commons.wikimedia.org/wiki/File:Viajes_de_col on_en.svg

In the next 12 years, Columbus conducted three more expeditions. On the second expedition, as he sailed westward along the east coast of Cuba, he was sure that this was what Marco Polo said about the coast of southern China. When the coast suddenly turned south, he knew he had come to Marco Polo's "Golden Peninsula": The Malay Archipelago.

Before the third expedition, it was already believed there might be a large continent to the west of the island discovered by Columbus (the island of Cuba), and that the continent was probably not Asia. However, Columbus did not believe it and was busy with his third expedition. This time, he discovered the Gulf of Paria in eastern Venezuela and the Orinoco River that flowed into this bay. He was shocked by the wideness and greatness of the gulf and rivers, and became more convinced that this was a "great continent".

During the 4th expedition, Columbus sailed southwest along the coast of Cuba until he reached the coast of the Atlantic (today in the Republic of Honduras). He then sailed east and south along the coast. He wanted to find the strait to enter the Indian Ocean as mentioned by Marco Polo (the Strait of Malacca). Although no straits had ever been found in this region, Columbus still did not give up his assumption he had arrived in Asia. He

Assumption 1. Confirmed Ideas Are Solid and True

simply believed the golden peninsula may be longer than originally expected. As long as he sailed far enough to the south, he would surely find a way to the strait into the Indian Ocean.

During these four expeditions, Columbus explained away all the evidence against his assumption that he had reached Asia. He only collected and believed information consistent with his hypothesis.

If he had jumped out of his thoughts and then sailed along the coast of Cuba for a while, he would discover Cuba was only an island and not mainland China. Unfortunately, Columbus failed to do so and believed he reached Asia until his death.

Another navigator, Amerigo Vespucci, did not follow Columbus's thinking and steps. Vespucci first suggested the idea that the continent Columbus discovered was another one outside Europe, Asia, and Africa. The New World, therefore, was finally named after Amerigo Vespucci rather than Christopher Columbus: America.

On the issue of where the New World really was, Columbus actually entered a "confirmation bias". Confirmation bias is a thinking bias that arises from one fundamental assumption of our mind. That is, confirmed ideas are solid and true.

When being confirmed of our viewpoints, we feel happy and assured because we assume that confirmed ideas are solid and true. However, once we have formed a viewpoint, we are inclined to seek out and embrace information that confirms that viewpoint. Meanwhile, information that casts doubt on it is easily ignored and misinterpreted in a self-serving manner.

Like wishful thinking, we tend to pick up information that makes us feel good because they confirm our assumptions. This guides us into a sampling bias, just like a blind man who touches but a part of an elephant (see Figure 1-3).

Figure 1-3 Blind Men Touch an Elephant. If one happens to reach the elephant's side, he believes it is like a wall; if one happens to reach the leg, he believes it is like a pillar; if one happens to reach the ear, he believes it is like a fan.

This sampling bias reduces the likelihood that our expectations and assumptions will be overturned. As a result, just like Columbus, we become the prisoners of our assumptions. Confirmation bias stems from the "confirmation" strategy we use for reasoning.

The Confirmation Strategy We Use and Why to Reject and Falsify It

Take a few minutes to think about the following task.

Look at this set of figures, 2-4-6. This set of numbers is in line with a hidden rule and your goal is to discover it. In order to find out what that rule is, you need to come up with a new set of numbers to test the rules you come up with. Every time you come up with a new set of numbers, I will tell you if it is in line with the rule. If you think you have found the rule, stop to tell me what the rule is.

What do you think? Or, what kind of figures would you come up with?

You may guess this is a set of increasing even numbers, so you test it with 4-8-10. Then I tell you the numbers you come up with is correct. What will you do next? Use 6-8-12 again to test it? I will tell you again that this set of figures is correct.

After testing several sets of even numbers and receiving positive feedback each time, perhaps you—in fact, most people—will feel confident that the rule behind this set of numbers is a set of increasing *even* numbers, and then stop thinking/testing.

But what if I tell you the rule is actually "a set of increasing numbers"?

Karl Popper, a 20th-century philosopher of science, believed one mistake that people often make is thinking about "confirming" instead of "rejecting" their assumptions. That is, everyone thinks how to go about with "confirmation" instead of "falsification". The latter means looking for counterexamples.

Interestingly enough, other scholars criticized Popper and thought that he advocated falsification and self-negation, when he himself was aggressive and confident in advocating falsification strategies. It is said that in Popper's class, some students asked him whether people could "falsify falsification". Popper said if someone dared to ask such a clever question again, he would throw him out of the class.

Assumption 1. Confirmed Ideas Are Solid and True

Figure 1-4 Karl Popper

One of Popper's students, Peter C. Wason, a cognitive psychologist, designed the above task to study the deviations that occur when people test their hypotheses. In this task, people usually start by assuming the rule here is a set of increasing *even* numbers and then try to think of multiple sets of numbers to confirm this rule. Thanks to continued positive feedback, people stop thinking and believe they have found the correct answer. However, they are wrong.

The correct rule is simply a set of increasing numbers. The set of increasing *even* numbers people think of is only a subset of the correct rule. If people come up with a set of numbers such as 4-5-6 to see if they would reject their assumptions, they would immediately find the correct rule.

From this example, we can clearly see that even if our ideas are confirmed, they are not necessarily correct. However, people use the confirmation strategy in their daily lives almost all the time (examples below).

As a result, people's strategy to confirm their own expectations and assumptions reduces the likelihood these expectations and assumptions will be overturned. This leads them to confirmation bias. Information consistent with our expectations and assumptions is more likely to be noticed, memorized, recalled, and processed by the brain compared to inconsistent information. We also perceive ambiguous information according to our initial expectations. This guides us into a sampling trap and brings about wrong judgments and decisions.

It was confirmation bias that made Columbus the slave of his dream. Columbus collected evidence supporting his notion that the land he discovered was Asia. He explained away all the evidence against his hypothesis and merely trusted the information consistent with his hypothesis. Therefore, it is perhaps better to call his four exploration trips to the New World four "confirmation trips".

The Hypothetico-Deductive Method for Reasoning

The scientific revolution led by Copernicus in the 16th century was followed by a number of eminent scientists including Galileo Galilei, Francis Bacon, William Harvey, Rene Descartes, Isaac Newton, John Herschel, William Whewell, and John Stuart Mill. After three centuries of development, in the middle of the 19th century, at the time when Darwin and Wallace proposed the theory of evolution by natural selection, the scientific method finally became known as the Hypothetico-Deductive Method, which is still widely used today.

According to this hypothetico-deductive method (see Figure 1-5), scientists first generalize a hypothesis based on their observations, which can be from their own experiences or from others' previous studies. They then deduct some conclusions or predictions from this hypothesis. Finally, they test these conclusions through observation and experimentation. If the deducted conclusions or predictions are valid, then the initial hypothesis is correct and is accepted as a rule.

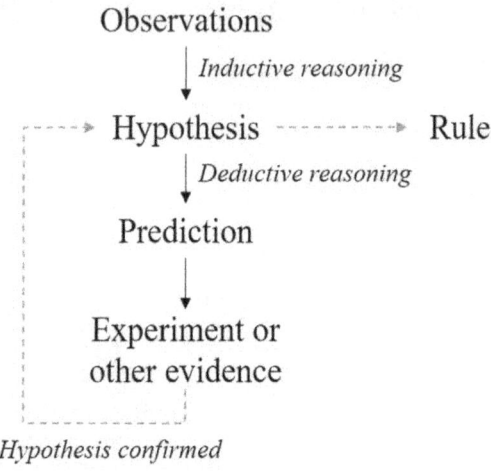

Figure 1-5 The Hypothetico-Deductive Method

Darwin and Wallace used this hypothetico-deductive method for their research. Taking Darwin as an example, he proceeded from the process of artificial selection of domesticated animals and the evidence he collected during the *HMS Beagle* voyage and inducted the hypothesis that species evolve in nature through natural selection. He then deductively reasoned that the evolution of each species is subject to natural selection, and finally collected evidence of various species to see whether it is true or not.

This hypothetico-deductive method is essentially an inductive reasoning. It is one way of making broad generalizations from specific observations. However, as people often use confirmation strategies, validation using the hypothetico-deductive method may lead to confirmation bias, just like Columbus and the mistakes people made in the task above.

It should be noted that I am not saying we should abandon the hypothetico-deductive method, but instead we should be more careful when using it. Each time, we should strive to falsify our assumptions in order to reach more sound conclusions.

Confirmation Biases in Psychologists

One study surveyed over 700 psychologists and found that they tended to rate research findings based on their own academic opinions. Findings consistent with their academic opinions were rated more credible and the corresponding research methods more rigorous, compared to findings inconsistent with their academic opinions. This was especially true in research related to controversial topics.

In another study, researchers created two reports using the same research method but with opposite results and conclusions. They then sent the reports to 75 reviewers of a famous psychological journal and solicited their opinions. As a result, the reviewers tended to answer "acceptance" or "minor revision" when reading results consistent with their own academic views. In contrast, when reading results against their academic views, they tended to answer "rejection" or "major revision".

Interestingly, in this study, the researchers included one artificial mistake in the reports. In the methodology section, there was a sentence that read "a total of 8 subjects were evenly divided into 3 groups". Obviously, it was impossible. In the results section, the correct number of subjects was shown in a table, suggesting there were totally 12 subjects. It turned out that only 25% of reviewers found this mistake when the study results were consistent with their own academic views. However, 71.4% of reviewers found this mistake when the results were inconsistent with their own academic views.

Why did the reviewers become more "serious" when reading research findings inconsistent with their own academic views, and were better able to pick out mistakes? Likely, confirmation bias was working here.

When reading findings consistent with their own views, the reviewers' expectations were confirmed and they felt the results were authentic and trustworthy. There was no incentive to look at other evidence

Assumption 1. Confirmed Ideas Are Solid and True

carefully, so it was easy for them to ignore the mistake. When reading findings inconsistent with their own opinions, the reviewers assumed the study was problematic and questioned the methodology of the study. They would, therefore, spend more time scrutinizing other information and find the error more easily.

For academically controversial topics, this confirmation bias may be important, because it allows scholars to look at problems more closely and reach more trustworthy conclusions.

However, confirmation bias harms discoveries and innovation. The feedback given by reviewers or peer review experts under the influence of confirmation bias is no longer accurate. At the same time, the reviewers' negative opinions given to research findings inconsistent with their own opinions will undermine the enthusiasm of researchers, hinder them from publishing their findings and delay the spread of new discoveries.

Indeed, a survey of 16 top journal editors belonging to the American Psychological Association found that very few researchers are willing to submit on controversial topics, and most of those articles submitted will not receive approval from reviewers. Of course, reviewers will not explicitly say they disagree with these findings. Rather, like the reviewers reported in the study above, many of them will find other flaws in these studies.

Confirmation Biases in Medical Doctors

In *The Tale of Two Minds: The Art and Science of Decision-making in Everyday Life*, I discussed how experienced medical doctors form hypotheses about the diagnosis shortly after interviewing patients. They then continue to collect information and verify their hypotheses. This begs the question: will the doctors be affected by confirmation bias?

The answer is yes. Confirmation bias compromises clinical decision-making. Let us look at a case-diagnosis study conducted with 75 psychiatrists. These psychiatrists had worked 6 years after their residency training.

Researchers artificially designed a case of Alzheimer's disease, but the initial case description was easily confused with major depressive disorder (depression). Generally, after reading the description of the patients, doctors perceive it as depression. Here is the case.

Assumption 1. Confirmed Ideas Are Solid and True

Patient, male, 65 years old, was sedated when admitted to hospital and was suspected of taking a large dose of sleeping pills.

The next day, the patient was fully awake and stated that he had been married for 32 years and lived in the city with his wife. He originally worked as an accountant at an electrical company and retired two years ago. He said he used to be happy and cheerful, but now he often felt lost and sad.

The patient's appearance was clean and tidy, but he looked depressed.

After reading this case and writing a preliminary diagnosis, the researchers gave the doctors 12 additional sets of information. Each set contained one short and one detailed message. The short message was an abstract of the detailed one. However, the psychiatrists could only see the short messages while they had to ask the researchers to show them the corresponding detailed messages.

The short messages were manipulated in a way that 6 of them seemed to support the diagnosis of depression, for instance, *the patient mentioned death in his conversation.* The remaining 6 short messages appeared to support the diagnosis of Alzheimer's disease, for instance, *the patient had memory problems*. However, what these doctors did not know was that the 12 detailed messages supported the diagnosis of Alzheimer's disease instead of depression.

Therefore, mimicking the process of a typical diagnostic interview, these doctors needed to further understand the detailed information behind the 12 short messages and see what type of diagnosis the overall evidence indicated. Doctors were free to ask the researchers for any number of detailed information based on the 12 short messages. After the information was requested, the doctors needed to make a final diagnosis.

By checking how the doctors sought further information to understand the patient's condition, researchers could see whether the doctors were able to correct their initial disease assumptions. The researchers could also know whether the doctors collected more information consistent with their initial hypothesis—that is, whether they would be affected by confirmation bias.

As expected, immediately after reading the case description, 73 of the 75 doctors (97%) made a preliminary diagnosis of depression, while only 2 (3%) considered Alzheimer's disease. In the process of requesting further information, 10 doctors (13%) focused on collecting information that was consistent with their initial hypothesis. For example, a doctor who believed that the initial diagnosis was depression specifically asked the information about how the patient mentioned death. In other words, 13% of the doctors showed confirmation bias.

The remaining 65 doctors (87%) either collected an equal amount of information for the two diseases or gathered more information about the other disease. For example, a doctor who believed the initial diagnosis was depression asked about the patient's memory functions. Therefore, we can think these doctors did not show confirmation bias.

As a result, among the 10 doctors who displayed confirmation bias, only 3 (30%) made a final correct diagnosis (Alzheimer's disease). Among the 65 doctors who did not show confirmation bias, 41 (63%) made a correct diagnosis. Therefore, confirmation bias reduces the accuracy of judgments.

Confirmation Biases in Our Everyday Lives

Confirmation bias largely misleads our intuition in our daily lives. Many people continue to smoke and drink heavily because they have come across people who smoke and drink heavily and yet still live healthily and happily. In sharp contrast, they frequently see or hear people die and develop various cancers despite not smoking and drinking at all. These examples confirm to them that smoking and drinking are not that bad.

Unfortunately, what they overlook is the whole picture which undoubtedly indicates smoking and drinking make people more vulnerable to a large number of diseases.

As another example, in the social context, our attitude and belief about other people are easily influenced by the initial information we obtained about them, or our first impressions. If we are going to meet a little girl born into a rich family, then we may expect her to have a very high talent and be able to dance gracefully. If she belongs to a poor family, our expectation may be quite the opposite.

Similarly, if we learn that a lady is a librarian, we are likely to think she is introverted and does not enjoy communication with others. However, if she is a real estate sales representative, we are more inclined to think that she is outgoing and good at communication. Although logically we know this is a typical social

Assumption 1. Confirmed Ideas Are Solid and True

stereotype (prejudice), we often automatically think in such a way.

A bit of information about an individual gives us some kind of expectation, and this expectation will inevitably affect our reactions when we come in contact with them. We are more likely to notice, perceive and recall information in accordance with our expectations. Such information is also considered more trustable.

In one study, psychologists had two groups of college students watch a video of a 4th-grade girl participating in an oral test. This was an ambiguous video. The girl answered half of the simple as well as difficult questions right and missed the other half. Half of the time, the girl was focused and able to speak and respond actively; the other half of the time, she was inattentive, did not talk much, and responded slowly. Interestingly, the first group of students had previously watched a video of the girl living in a poor area, while the second group had watched a video of her living in a rich area.

As a result, compared with the first group, the second group of students evaluated the young girl to answer more questions correct. They also tended to think she had more humanistic knowledge, higher reading and mathematics performance, better cognitive thinking skills, and higher creative potential. Her popularity and willingness to cooperate with others were considered higher and her psychological traits more mature.

A student in the first group commented that the girl "is not good at receiving new information". On the contrary, a student in the second group commented that she "has the ability to apply what she knows to unfamiliar situations".

The videos of the poor or rich family that the two groups of students watched beforehand gave them specific expectations of the girl. Like the reviewers we just discussed and Columbus who believed he had reached Asia, they unconsciously entered confirmation bias and selectively interpreted the girl's performance.

So far, the confirmation bias we have introduced is people forming a hypothesis or expectation first and then accordingly attending to the information in the external environment. However, there is another case.

People have already had information (attention, perception, and judgment) of things in their mind, then for some reason, they reach a new conclusion about those things. Later, people will use this new conclusion to recall information that has been originally stored. In this

Assumption 1. Confirmed Ideas Are Solid and True

case, confirmation bias is considered a selective recall of memory from their mind.

For instance, you once met with person A. Later, person B talks about A and evaluates him in a specific way. Then your subsequent recall of A will be affected by B's evaluation. It becomes easier for you to recall information that is consistent with B's judgment. Confirmation bias.

In another study, subjects learned about the typical life of a specific woman in a week. On the whole, the woman showed the same introverted and extroverted behaviors. She was active and cheerful when communicating with doctors, but introverted and did not love to socialize with strangers in a cafe shop. She chatted with strangers while jogging, but behaved timidly when shopping in the supermarket.

Then subjects were informed that the woman was currently applying for a job, half of whom were told she was applying for a librarian, and the other half a real estate sales representative. As a result, when later asked to recall the woman's behavior, subjects being told the woman applied for a librarian position on average recalled 6.8 of her introverted behaviors but only 3.4 of her extroverted behaviors. In contrast, subjects being told the woman applied for a job as a real estate sales representative on average recalled 5.9 of her extroverted behaviors but 3.8 of her introverted behaviors.

This sort of confirmation bias restrains us from processing information in a comprehensive and balanced manner. This often leads us to wrong conclusions and suboptimal decisions.

Avoiding Confirmation Bias

In order to avoid confirmation bias, we should first remind ourselves that the assumption that confirmed ideas are solid and true is actually incorrect and dangerous. We need to seek all available information and understand the overall situation and we should be especially careful about observations and facts that contradict with our own ideas or assumptions.

At the same time, we should revise our confirmation strategy and use the falsification strategy advocated by Karl Popper. Instead of looking for information that confirms our hypotheses, we gather information that rejects our hypothesis. When we find that information, we should take it seriously. Being objective and open-minded is the key to critical thinking and optimal decision-making.

Assumption 2. "Handsome Soldiers Are Good at Shooting"

While reading an article published in the renowned journal *Science* at graduate school, I found that the experimental methods contained in the supplementary materials conflicted with those described in the main text. So, I wrote to the corresponding author to inquire which was true. Two days later, the author seemed to be very embarrassed and replied, "Sorry, that was actually a mistake."

Science is unarguably one of the top academic journals. Every scientist dreams of publishing an article on it. However, there are even mistakes in articles published in *Science*. "*Science* is no more than that; there are errors in the experimental methods, can the conclusions of the research be correct?" That was my first reaction and subsequently the "halo" surrounding *Science* in my mind faded.

Of course, after I calmed down a bit, I realized that *Science* is still a scientific journal representing the highest level in the world, and the authors' conclusions in that study may still be credible. After that paper, over a hundred studies have verified their findings. However, the error I noticed at that time seemed to completely negate the authority and prestigious image of *Science* in my mind.

Why did I have such an intense reaction? Why was a small mistake so significant?

The Halo Effect

During World War I, as an army psychologist, Edward Lee Thorndike asked officers to evaluate various performances of soldiers, including their levels of intelligence, physical strength, leadership, and morality. Thorndike noticed an interesting phenomenon:

"It was as if officers figured that a soldier who was handsome and had good posture should also be able to shoot straight, polish his shoes well, and play the harmonica, too."

In a similar way, once a soldier was considered "a good fighter", the officers evaluated all aspects of the soldier as excellent.

This phenomenon also shows up frequently nowadays in the work setting when a supervisor evaluates a subordinate's job performance. It is very likely that the supervisor may give prominence to a single characteristic of the subordinate, for instance,

Assumption 2. "Handsome Soldiers Are Good at Shooting"

enthusiasm or likableness, and judge the entire subordinate based on that single characteristic.

A specific aspect of a person or object may bring us certain emotional reactions. Here, handsomeness, enthusiasm, and likeableness give people positive emotional reactions. These emotional reactions give people certain kinds of expectations. We automatically associate and relate this aspect to other aspects. Thorndike called this phenomenon "the halo effect".

Specifically, if we initially obtain certain positive information about something, then we tend to like it in general. We form a positive halo about it and think that all aspects of that thing are good. Conversely, if we initially get certain negative information on something, we dislike or even hate it. We form a negative halo about it and think that it is bad in almost all aspects. This kind of expectation is the halo effect.

Often, the halo effect affects our subsequent information processing. We are more likely to attend to information consistent with our initial expectation and neglect those inconsistent with it. The halo effect causes selective information processing and leads us to confirmation bias.

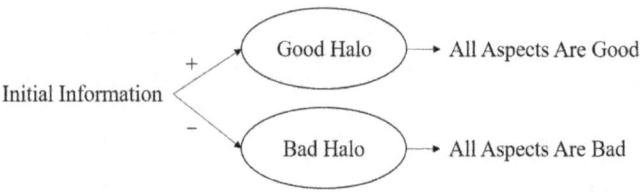

Figure 2-1 The Halo Effect

If a person is kind and friendly to us, we tend to like him/her. Under the influence of the halo effect, we will like his/her other characteristics including appearance, speaking habits, walking postures, and so on. "Love me, love my dog," and "Beauty is in the eyes of the beholder" are typical examples. Similarly, if a person is indifferent or even hostile towards us, we tend to dislike or hate him/her and his/her other characteristics. This may seem immature, but it does occur to many or even most of us.

In one study, psychologists asked people to watch a college teacher's interview video and then evaluate his appearance and the attractiveness of his English accent. However, psychologists created two versions of the same video. In one version, the teacher appeared enthusiastic and friendly; in the other, he seemed indifferent and asocial. His accent, however, was consistent and never changed. After watching the video, people who watched the enthusiastic and friendly video commented that the teacher was handsome and his accent attractive. In contrast, people who watched the indifferent and asocial video commented that the teacher and his accent was annoying. Under the influence of the halo effect, the same person gave people different impressions.

The halo effect also occurs in the classroom when teachers evaluate their students. A teacher who sees a first year student with high scores in the entrance exam may assume he is also diligent, well-behaved, and kind before the teacher has objectively evaluated the student in these dimensions.

Similarly, from the perspective of the halo effect, we can also easily understand the observations in the previous chapter. Psychologists who read research findings consistent with their own academic opinions tended to evaluate the research method being more rigorous and credible. They were also less likely to notice mistakes in the paper. The "logic" of the psychologists here was simple. Research with results consistent with one's own view formed a good halo, as a result, its method was also good. Research with results inconsistent with one's own view formed a bad halo, as a result, its method was also bad.

In the same tone, my reactions to *Science* earlier was also affected by the halo effect. Initially, *Science* formed a "perfect halo" in my mind. Papers published in the journal were believed flawless. Unfortunately, one mistake broke this halo and turned it to a disappointing, negative one. In fact, not only me, but Charles Darwin seemed to have been affected by the halo effect too.

Too High an Expectation Causes Disappointment

In the final year at Cambridge, Darwin read two books that inspired his interest in studying natural philosophy. One was *A Preliminary Discourse on the Study of Natural Philosophy* by John Herschel and the other *Personal Narrative of a Journey to the Equinoctial Regions of the New Continent* by Alexander von Humboldt.

While as a naturalist on the British Navy survey ship *HMS Beagle*, Darwin spent a lot of time exploring the places von Humboldt was interested in. Darwin's experience in South America confirmed the description and interpretation by von Humboldt in the *Personal Narrative of a Journey to the Equinoctial Regions of the New Continent*. Darwin wrote in his diary in February 1832, "*From what I have seen, Humboldt's glorious descriptions are and will forever be unparalleled...I am at present fit only to read Humboldt; he like another sun illumines everything I behold.*"

Assumption 2. "Handsome Soldiers Are Good at Shooting"

In a letter to his teacher, John Henslow, in May, the same year, Darwin further wrote: *"I formerly admired Humboldt, I now almost adore him; he alone gives any notion, of the feelings which are raised in the mind on first entering the Tropics."* Apparently, von Humboldt had formed a perfect halo in Darwin.

Later, when Darwin returned to England after his expedition and published five volumes of the series *The Zoology of the Voyage of HMS Beagle*, *"I once met at breakfast at Sir R. Murchison's house the illustrious Humboldt, who honoured me by expressing a wish to see me. I was a little disappointed with the great man, but my anticipations probably were too high. I can remember nothing distinctly about our interview, except that Humboldt was very cheerful and talked much."*

After meeting with von Humboldt in person, the perfect halo Darwin formed was shattered, so he felt "a little disappointed". This is a characteristic of our mind, or more specifically, the intuitive mind. It makes holistic evaluations and judgments to achieve overall harmony. This tendency appears automatically, strongly, and drives the halo effect.

Put it in a different way, the halo effect rests on our assumption that good things are good in general and bad things are bad in general, or "handsome soldiers are good at shooting". Since childhood, we have been taught a great lesson about good and bad people. Good people have good qualities in all domains while bad people stay bad in all aspects. We have been taught to behave like good people in every aspect. Although eventually, we realize that everyone has good qualities as well as bad ones.

But our intuition is unable to think in that "complex" way. It can only produce simple, consistent conclusions. It can only make associations based on existing information and form a single, overall impression and expectation. As a result, in daily life, we are haunted by the halo effect.

The Illusion of Business: Cisco's Story

Since John Chambers took over as CEO in 1995, Cisco had grown rapidly. By 1998, Cisco had occupied 40% of the market share of the networking hardware industry. The annual revenue had reached 8.5 billion U.S. dollars, which was 6 times that of 1995. The stock price also rose from less than 2 dollars per share at the beginning of 1995 to more than 20 dollars. In March 2000, Cisco's stock even soared to 80 dollars per share and its market

Assumption 2. "Handsome Soldiers Are Good at Shooting"

value reached 555 billion dollars, surpassing Microsoft to become the world's highest market value company.

During this period, even John Chambers' "legendary experience" was documented by business observers. In May 2000, *Fortune* magazine published a cover story "There's Something About Cisco". In this six-page long article, the authors wrote: *"The point is that Cisco, with CEO John Chambers at the helm, must now be considered one of America's truly outstanding companies, in the same league as Intel, Wal-Mart, and, yes, GE."*

However, as the economic growth slowed down, Cisco's stock and market value fell. At the end of 2000, Cisco's stock dropped to 38 dollars per share, and the market value fell back to 367 billion dollars. In April 2001, its stock further fell to 14 dollars per share, and the market value 140 billion dollars. In other words, Cisco's market value evaporated more than 400 billion dollars in a year.

The following month, "Cisco Fractures Its Own Fairy Tale" immediately appeared in *Fortune* magazine. *"Those looking for someone to blame can start with a CEO who didn't seem able to turn off the spigot of his own optimism... Basking in such a culture of confidence,*

Chambers and his managers seem to have had difficulty anticipating bad news and forecasting lower demand for their company's products…Acquisitions, forecasting, technology, and, yes, senior management…all have failed Cisco in the past year."

In September 2002, the stock price fell below $10 per share, and the market value 100 billion. After that, Cisco began to recover slowly. By 2003, there had been a marked improvement. In October 2003, the stock price had risen to 20 dollars per share. In the third quarter, the market value had returned to 134 billion. The market value in the fourth quarter became further higher. It reached nearly 154 billion dollars.

In November 2003, *Business Weekly* published the cover title "Cisco's Comeback". *"After an initial period of denial, CEO Chambers seized on the tech slump as an opportunity to rethink every aspect of the company. Now, the once-sullied highflier is stronger than ever. How did Chambers and his team pull it off?"*

Like the phenomenon of Cisco, when a company is profitable, managers, journalists, professors, and other business observers automatically consider the company's strategies, corporate cultures, leadership, values, customer services and so on as all being great.

Profits give the company a glorious "perfect halo". Once the company's revenue declines and the bubble bursts, the attitude of observers turns 180 degrees: nothing of this company is good anymore.

Risks and Benefits Under the Halo Effect

We know that risks and benefits are two separate concepts. In general, things have both risks and benefits. In everyday life, the risk of something that can bring significant benefits is either small or large. The risk of things that can bring small gains will generally be smaller, otherwise, they will be abandoned. Therefore, as a general rule of thumb, the (potential) benefits of high-risk things should be higher than those of low-risk things.

Taking the automobile as an example, no one would deny the great convenience it brings to our lives. Cars can be regarded as a major advancement in the history of human civilization. But at the same time, cars also pose great risks—traffic accidents kill millions a year.

Another example is nuclear power. According to the International Atomic Energy Agency, 17% of the world's electricity comes from nuclear energy. France's nuclear power accounts for even 78% of its electricity. However, the risk of nuclear power is equally huge, such as the nuclear leak of the three-mile island in the United

States in 1979, the Chernobyl nuclear leakage in the Soviet Union in 1986, and the nuclear accident in Fukushima of Japan in 2011.

Therefore, statistically speaking, if there is a correlation between the benefit and the risk of things, the correlation should be positive (see Figure 2-2).

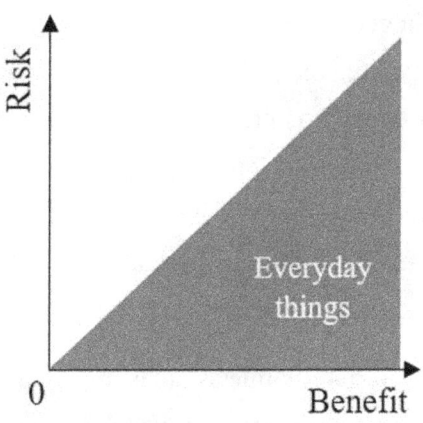

Figure 2-2 The Risk and Benefit of Everyday Things.

However, people do not think in this way. People's subjective perception of risk and benefit is influenced by the halo effect.

Paul Slovic, a psychologist at the University of Oregon, asked people to quickly evaluate the benefits and risks of many everyday life items. Cars, mobile phones, beef, tobacco, alcohol, pesticides, natural gas,

Assumption 2. "Handsome Soldiers Are Good at Shooting"

food preservatives, chemical fertilizers, chemical factories, explosives, and drinking water, a full list of those things was given to people for evaluation. Interestingly, people's evaluation of the benefits of these items was negatively correlated with the risks (correlation coefficients range from -0.71 to -0.36, which were impressive). They believed that the greater the benefit, the smaller the risk; the greater the risk, the smaller the benefit. However, whereas these items do have big benefits, most of them are accompanied by huge risks.

Under the influence of the halo effect, people's perception of risk depends on their initial pool of information or their initial impression. If people initially profited from a certain object or gained information about its benefit, they usually form positive attitudes toward that object. Positive attitudes bring a positive halo, and people often think the risk of the object is quite small. For example, most people think vaccines, antibodies, electricity, and X-rays have large profits and low risks.

On the contrary, if people initially received negative information about something, for instance, something being highly dangerous, they will form negative attitudes towards it. They tend to think the profit of that thing is also small. Many people believe that alcohol, tobacco, insecticides, aviation, and firearms, have a high risk and low benefit. But ask anyone who drinks alcohol or smokes how they feel after one consumption. The immediate pleasure is impressive, isn't it?

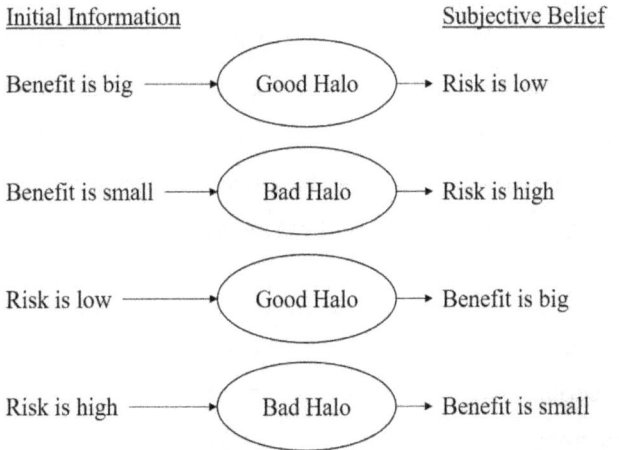

Figure 2-3 People's Perception of Risk and Benefit under the Halo Effect

In another study, Slovic asked people to evaluate the benefits and risks of nuclear energy, natural gas, and food preservatives. He then showed half of them an article describing the low-risk characteristic of these things, while showing the other half an article describing the high-risk characteristic of these things. Later, when asked to rate the benefits of these things again, those who read the low-risk article tended to assess their benefits as big. In contrast, those who read the high-risk article tended to evaluate their benefits being small.

Similarly, when people read articles saying that the benefits of nuclear energy, natural gas, and food preservatives are big, they consider their risks being low. When people read articles saying these things are of small benefit, they consider their risks being high.

Two studies have captured the change of people's attitude towards nuclear powers following the Chernobyl and the Fukushima nuclear leakages, providing further support for our discussion here. Two months before the Chernobyl nuclear leak, a Dutch researcher investigated Dutch people's attitudes towards nuclear powers. One month after the leak, the researcher interviewed those people again. It turned out that compared to before the leak, people rated the risk of nuclear powers (the probability of nuclear leakage) being higher and the benefit being smaller after the leak.

Similarly, five months before the Fukushima nuclear power accident, a Swiss study investigated Swiss people's perceptions of nuclear power. Immediately after the accident, the researchers investigated people's attitudes again. Compared to before the accident, people considered nuclear power being of higher risk and lower benefit after the accident. Meanwhile, they rated nuclear power scientists, energy management departments, and nuclear power plant operators less trustworthy.

Under the influence of the halo effect, people's perception of risk and benefit is no longer accurate. More importantly, not only ordinary people, professionals who have received much training in the field of business and economics seem to be also affected by the halo effect.

In one study, economists asked 742 stock analysts and investment advisers to predict the expected returns of a list of stocks in the coming five years. They were told to make their predictions based on four risk indicators: leverage, growth prospects, stock liquidity, and analyst coverage. Despite their professional experience, these analysts and advisers predicted that the higher the risk of a stock, the lower the returns it possesses; the lower the risk of a stock, the higher the returns it possesses. However, the actual returns of these stocks are positively related to their risk. The greater the returns, the higher the risk. The smaller the return, the lower the risk.

As people are willing to pay higher prices to buy stocks with large profits but low risk, it will eventually reduce the stock returns. But the experts seem not to realize this. Their "professional" judgments are influenced by their attitudes, or by the halo effect.

Overcoming the Halo Effect

George Bernard Shaw once said, "Love is a gross exaggeration of the difference between one person and everybody else." This exaggeration is actually based on the halo effect. This is a fundamental characteristic of the human mind, that we tend to form overall, homogenous expectations about things and these expectations are typically in either a positive or negative way.

In the case of love and marriage, we know that an immature halo is harmful. Based on limited, initial information of another person, we can hardly make optimal decisions. The preferred strategy here is to gather enough information about another person, for instance, by going out with him/her for a while and understanding each other. After that, if you still feel good about him/her, then that is an informed halo and you can trust it.

Put it in another way, if a couple acts solely based on the good halo each other formed with their limited, initial information of each other, their good halo will fade into a bad one. However, if their halo is a result of their deep understanding of each other, it is great for their love and future. It binds them together and helps them resolve many everyday conflicts.

Nevertheless, in the light of rational decision making in everyday life, particularly in the financial and social world, the halo effect is harmful. No one wants to be deceived by halos.

The halo effect is an intuitive reaction. It is based on our innate assumption that good things are good in general, or "handsome soldiers are good at shooting".

As we have discussed extensively in *The Tale of Two Minds: The Art and Science of Decision-making in Everyday Life*, intuition is fast, effortless, and helps us deal with many issues in our daily lives. However, they also cause impulsive decision-making and problems in many situations.

What we can do to combat this is to use our rational mind to correct this intuition. We must question and go beyond our innate assumption that good things are good in general. We have to look at things from different aspects and not in a rushed manner. What concerns us is the aspect or issue itself, not the person or thing in general.

Assumption 2. "Handsome Soldiers Are Good at Shooting"

In cases when making final overall judgments, we should gather sufficient information from different aspects and then process that information in a comprehensive and objective manner.

Psychologists found that a training lasting merely five minutes with managers can reduce the influence of the halo effect in their evaluation of employees' performance. The five minutes contained three steps: first, introducing the concept of the halo effect; second, giving a real example; and third, offering advice on how to overcome the halo effect, namely evaluating different aspects before making any overall judgments.

In this chapter alone, we have experienced far more than five minutes of training so you'll fare much better than these managers.

Assumption 3. Fluent Memories Are More Compelling and Trustable

"If I Cannot Recall It, It's Perhaps Not That True/Important…"

Please try to answer the following set of questions.

1. Recall 4 things that happened when you were a child.

    A.

    B.

    C.

    D.

2. Is there a lot of childhood things that you cannot remember?

    A. Yes

    B. Uncertain

    C. No

Good questions. They remind us of the good old days. Now, look at another set of questions.

1. Recall 12 things that happened when you were a child.

Assumption 3. Fluent Memories Are More Compelling and Trustable

A.

B.

C.

D.

E.

F.

G.

H.

I.

J.

K.

L.

2. Is there a lot of childhood things that you cannot remember?

A. Yes

B. Uncertain

C. No

These were actually questions used in an experiment conducted by social psychologist Norbert Schwarz at the University of Michigan. He asked people to answer one of the two sets of questions above and compared their responses. Surprisingly, whereas 19% of those who were asked to recall 4 childhood happenings subsequently acknowledged that they had lost many childhood memories (answered 'Yes' in the second question), 46% of those who were asked to recall 12 childhood happenings gave the same answer.

In other words, although the latter group of people recalled three times more childhood happenings, they were over twice as likely to admit that they had lost many childhood memories. Why?

In another experiment, Schwarz asked people to recall either 6 or 12 situations where they have displayed stubborn behavior, followed by a self-evaluation question of how stubborn they feel about themselves. On a scale of 0 to 10, those who recalled 6 stubborn scenes of themselves rated their own stubbornness on average of 6.3, while those who recalled 12 stubborn scenes gave an average rating of 5.2. Strange. People recalling more stubborn situations judged themselves less stubborn. What is going on here?

Assumption 3. Fluent Memories Are More Compelling and Trustable

If people can recall 12 things that happened in their childhood or daily lives, surely they can easily recall 4 or 6 when asked to. Therefore, the key here is unlikely to be the first 4 or 6 pieces of memory, but the additional ones they recall.

Put it simply, for the average person, recalling 12 childhood memories is more difficult than recalling 4, and recalling 12 stubborn scenes of themselves is more difficult than recalling 6. It is likely people use the difficulty of recalling memories to judge whether they have forgotten their childhood happenings and whether they are stubborn. What we can recall is certainly important, but the process of recalling that information matters too.

When people make judgments and decisions, they not only consider what they recall but also pay attention to the difficulty and ease of recalling those contents. That is to say, people usually use the "fluency" of memory retrieval as extra information for judgment and decision-making. The fluency of memory retrieval is our internal meta-cognitive cues about our own mental processes. It is also called "availability" by psychologists. Information with high availability is more fluent and easily available to the mind.

In general, the easier it is to retrieve a piece of information, the more important and representative people evaluate that information. Vice versa, "if I cannot recall it, perhaps it is not that important to me." This is another fundamental assumption of our mind.

Recalling 12 memories is more difficult than recalling 4 or 6, so people who recalled 12 childhood memories were more likely to think they lost a lot of childhood memories, and people who recalled 12 stubborn scenes were more likely to comment that they were not stubborn.

Sampling Traps

Somewhat disappointingly, from the perspective of information processing, the assumption that memory that is more fluent is more trustable is incorrect. As a matter of fact, information with high fluency—that easily comes to your mind—is not necessarily truly important and representative of the big picture.

This is actually the trick of memory. Information with stronger memory strength is more easily recalled and thus has higher fluency. But many irrelevant factors can affect memory strength and change the fluency of information. I have discussed extensively on the psychology and neuroscience of memory in *Strategic Memory: The Natural History of Learning and*

Assumption 3. Fluent Memories Are More Compelling and Trustable

Forgetting. Here, let's focus on the biasing part of memory.

As we can only use available memory for making judgments and decisions and we use the fluency of retrieval as additional information, this leads us to a sampling trap. Some memory, despite its importance, is perhaps unavailable at a certain moment, while others that easily come to your mind may turn out to be trivial.

One biasing factor is repetition. Repeated information has stronger memory strength and is more likely to be recalled. However, we know repeated information is not necessarily important. Ads, for instance. We come across various ads every day, on TV, during movies, and on our way to work/school and back home. But are those ads important to us? No.

An experiment by social psychologist Timothy Wilson made a good illustration of how we are easily manipulated by repetition. He first asked people to read a list describing a man's personality in a balanced way, which included 5 positive messages, 5 negative messages, and 4 neutral messages. Then he gave people a chance to review the list. However, the experiment was manipulated in such a way that some people only reviewed 3 positive messages and 2 neutral messages, while other people reviewed only 3 negative messages and 2 neutral messages. This simple manipulation turned out to be effective enough to change people's memory and fluency of information retrieval, leading them to a sampling trap.

It turns out that although the information people initially read was exactly the same, those who reviewed positive information evaluated the man more positively. In contrast, those who reviewed negative information rated the man more negatively.

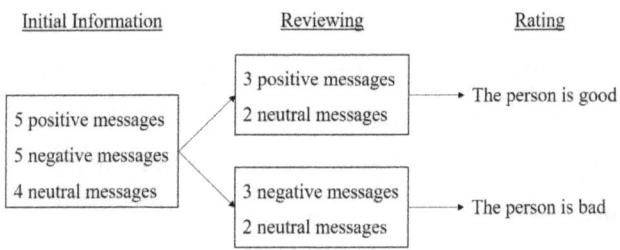

Figure 3-1 Sampling Traps Bias Judgment:
Wilson's Study

What Happens after a Man Views an Ad 20 Times?

Here is a piece of advice from London businessman Thomas Smith in 1885:

"The first time people look at any given ad, they don't even see it.

Assumption 3. Fluent Memories Are More Compelling and Trustable

The second time, they don't notice it.

The third time, they are aware that it is there.

The fourth time, they have a fleeting sense that they've seen it somewhere before.

The fifth time, they actually read the ad.

The sixth time, they thumb their nose at it.

The seventh time, they start to get a little irritated with it.

The eighth time, they start to think "Here's that confounded ad again."

The ninth time, they start to wonder if they may be missing out on something.

The tenth time, they ask their friends and neighbors if they've tried it.

The eleventh time, they wonder how the company is paying for all these ads.

The twelfth time, they start to think that it must be a good product.

The thirteenth time, they start to feel the product has value.

The fourteenth time, they start to remember wanting a product exactly like this for a long time.

The fifteenth time, they start to yearn for it because they can't afford to buy it.

The sixteenth time, they accept the fact that they will buy it sometime in the future.

The seventeenth time, they make a note to buy the product.

The eighteenth time, they curse their poverty for not allowing them to buy this terrific product.

The nineteenth time, they count their money very carefully.

The twentieth time prospects see the ad, they buy what it is offering."

Funny, isn't it?

Given repeated exposure, people will be convinced (themselves) to buy whatever you want them to buy. But why? Why is that possible?

The Mere Exposure Effect

Robert B. Zajonc, an American social psychologist, reported an observation in 1968 that, seeing or hearing

Assumption 3. Fluent Memories Are More Compelling and Trustable

something multiple times increases people's positive feelings towards those things. That is, people tend to like unfamiliar things they see or hear repeatedly.

In a series of experiments, Zajonc showed people several unfamiliar geometric figures, faces, and Chinese characters. When asked what they liked the most, people always tended to choose the ones that appeared the most. Zajonc called this phenomenon "the mere exposure effect".

Zajonc believed that the simple exposure effect is a result of the classical conditioning. Classical conditioning, also known as the Pavlovian conditioning, is a simple form of learning. It means that if an emotionally neutral thing appears with a positive stimulus (such as a reward) at the same time, we will develop positive feelings towards this thing.

For instance, when a sexy beauty stands next to a car, men tend to have a good impression of the car. The sexy beauty is a kind of reward, and the original emotionally neutral car becomes positive because of this reward. Similarly, in the simple exposure effect, Zajonc believed that if we encounter a stimulus (thing) many times and there are no aversive outcomes—bad things—happen, we will also have a good impression of this stimulus. No aversive events itself is a reward, like the sexy beauty above.

This interpretation is justified, but Zajonc ignored another important explanation: the fluency of information. Exposure to information will leave traces in people's memory and increase the fluency of that information. Information with high fluency can be processed more quickly when encountered again. It does not need much attention and effort compared to totally unfamiliar things, so it is more easily noticed and processed.

Crucially, we often assume this feeling of fluency represents familiarity, attractiveness, and trustworthiness. We further use this feeling for judgment and decision-making.

The bad news is, people usually don't recognize the source of their feelings, but always try to use rational thinking to explain them, which is called "rationalization".

Let's return to the story of the man who saw the same ad 20 times.

Assumption 3. Fluent Memories Are More Compelling and Trustable

"The fourth time, they have a fleeting sense that they've seen it somewhere before." The ad has left traces in the man's memory and its fluency gradually increased.

"The ninth time, they start to wonder if they may be missing out on something." Fluency began to bring about the rationalization process.

"The twelfth time, they start to think that it must be a good product." The rationalization process yielded a clear positive information.

"The seventeenth time, they make a note to buy the product." "The twentieth time prospects see the ad, they buy what it is offering." In the end, the mere exposure effect won.

"It must be a good product," "The product has value." This man's seemingly funny thought-pattern is a typical example of how people rationalize the feeling of mere exposure and fluency.

Human Kindness, or Thinking Bias?

I once read a "romantic" love story that happened in Taiwan. A young man wrote 700 letters to his beloved woman. The woman finally agreed to marry "him", but unfortunately "he" was the postman who delivered the 700 letters.

It is easy to understand this story's end. We often experience this ourselves. In daily life, even if we don't know a stranger, we will unavoidably develop a sense of intimacy and familiarity with them after seeing them several times.

This kind of feeling may not be the primary explanation for the above "romantic" story, but it likely initiated further communication between the postman and the woman. Imagine, who could be indifferent to someone they met 700 times?

Of course, this is not a coincidence. It is the result of the mere exposure effect and our mental assumptions that information that feels fluent is familiar and intimate to us.

Psychologists have found similar results through rigorously designed experiments. In one study, psychologists asked three similarly attractive women to attend a college course with 200 students. They attended 5, 10, and 15 classes, respectively, and did not communicate with any students during the classes.

At the end of the semester, psychologists took pictures of these three women together with another woman who had never attended the course, and let the students in this course evaluate their attractiveness. As

Assumption 3. Fluent Memories Are More Compelling and Trustable

you can guess, the woman who attended the course 15 times was rated most attractive, followed by the one who attended 10 and 5 times.

People develop good impressions of unfamiliar things that they see repeatedly. But this begs the question: is there anything wrong with this? Isn't this kind of intimacy the best interpretation of "humanity", "goodness", and "human kindness"?

It is true this kind of intimacy is commendable from the perspective of "humanity". But in the face of judgment and decision-making, mere exposure makes us prefer repeatedly seen or heard things. If you do not obtain accurate, comprehensive, and representative information of the target object, but only rely on your feelings brought about by mere exposure, it will inevitably lead to decision-making mistakes.

Take a singing contest as an example. The selection criteria of the singing contest should be the singing level of the players, but if a player, due to previous contact with the judges or audience, which created a sense of familiarity in the latter, gets higher evaluations or votes, that is not a human kindness, but a typical bias.

In fact, a 2012 study found that mere exposure did affect the audience's voting choices in the European

Song Contest. The European Song Contest is an annual competition where singers are selected by each country. The whole contest will be broadcasted live on TV. Audiences from all countries can vote by phone or SMS, but only for players from other countries. Finally, the host country will count the votes and rank.

After 2008, the European Song Contest has implemented new rules for the game. The competition consists of two semi-finals and one final. Players from all countries are divided into two semi-finals, and the winner will enter the finals (Figure 3-2).

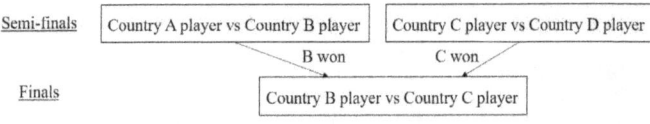

Figure 3-2 The European Song Contest

However, as depicted, this may create the mere exposure effect. Although people can't vote for players in their own country, they are more inclined to watch the semi-finals with their own national players, meaning that in the finals, people will see the same players they have seen in the semi-finals.

As a result, players from other countries that have played against the audience's country are more familiar, as opposed to players who did not appear in the semi-

Assumption 3. Fluent Memories Are More Compelling and Trustable

finals. As shown in Figure 3-2, the audience in Country A has two chances to meet the players in Country B, while the audience in Country D has two chances to meet the players in Country C. But, does this familiarity influence voting?

The answer was yes. Psychologists analyzed the results of the 2008-2011 European Song Contest final and found that the players generally got more votes from the audience in the countries where they won the semi-finals. That is, among Country B and C players, Country A audience will vote more for Country B players, while Country D audience will vote more for Country C players.

Just because they have met the player once in the semi-finals, people then voted for the player of being better at singing, which was totally against the true selection criteria. This kind of intimacy, or "human kindness", inadvertently influences people's judgments and rational decision-making abilities.

Be Careful What You Expose Yourself to

Be careful what you consume throughout your daily life. It will change your memory and fluency of information retrieval, which subsequently forms your preference and affects your judgment, unconsciously. This simple rule applies to many areas of our life.

Take watching TV and movies for instance. There is abundant evidence that repeated exposure to advertising and media violence causes behavioral changes in adults and children. Frequently reported changes include more alcohol drinking, smoking, consumption of junk foods, aggression, and fighting. The effect in children proves to be more evident, as they are still developing and learning to deal with their feelings and make rational decisions.

Just as the man's reaction to watching an ad 20 times, these repeated advertisements and media violence will increase the fluency of that information. Being more fluent makes them much easier to enter the decision-making process and change our judgment. This is certainly not what we want—although it is what the marketers want.

The mere exposure effect usually happens in the absence of specific information about unfamiliar things. It happens because we use the fluency of retrieval as additional information for making judgments and decisions. In order to avoid such influences, we need to revise our assumption and thoroughly understand the true criteria for judgment and decision-making. We should then comprehensively obtain information (accurate information) of the target objects in these standards.

Assumption 4. Being Simple and Salient Is Being Real and Special

Look at the following eight stock codes:

Alet, Barnings, Emniyet, Pera, Taahhut, Vander, Xagibdan, Yoalumnix

Based on your gut and best intuition, which do you think will perform well after being newly released to the stock market? Pick up four of them.

Perhaps, like most people, you may think Alet, Barnings, Pera, and Vander will outperform the other four stocks. Won't you?

Why? Because they are simpler and easier to read. They are pronounceable while the others are not.

"Fluent" Stocks Make More Money

Psychologist Daniel M. Oppenheimer at Princeton University asked people to predict the stock fluctuations of a list of unfamiliar companies. Compared to companies with a complex stock code, people always thought the stocks of companies with an easy-to-read code would perform better.

In order to understand whether this phenomenon occurs in real-life stock trading, Oppenheimer studied

665 stocks released in the New York Stock Exchange and 116 stocks released in the American Stock Exchange from 1990 to 2004. He divided all the stocks into two groups, one whose code was pronounceable (like KARs) and one whose code could not be directly pronounced until we add vowels in (such as RDO). He then calculated each group's future returns.

Surprisingly, compared to stocks whose code was unpronounceable, stocks whose code was pronounceable earned 8.54% more on the first day, 4.24% more after one week, 3.71% more after 6 months, and 2.03% more after one year.

Among newly released stocks, people generally do not have sufficient information to judge their real value. They have to use all their available knowledge to predict the stocks' future performance. The characteristic of the stock codes turns out to be one such information that is easily picked up by people—unconsciously at no cost.

Being simple is being fluent. Simple codes are easily perceived and processed by our brains. More fluent information feels better, more familiar, and more trustworthy. This is another assumption of our mind. "If something is fluent, it may be special." This assumption is just like our assumption about the fluency of recalling or information retrieval.

Assumption 4. Being Simple and Salient Is Being Real and Special

The fluency effect—let's call it this—is a psychological phenomenon that exists in many aspects of our lives. Its major underlying mechanism is that the capacity of our brain to process information is limited and therefore simpler things are easier for our brain to process. Hence the saying "simplicity is beauty".

Although it is but a simple feeling, it is likely to initiate a series of rationalizations or cognitive (mis)explanations. One such explanation might be that executives of those easy-to-read stock codes are smarter and more professional.

Notably, the return of those stocks decreased over time, from 8.54% on the first day to 2.03% a year later, which weakens the latter explanation. However, the truth may be more like this: as people's knowledge of the newly released stocks increased, they pay more attention to the profitability and risk indicators of those stocks—instead of their naïve, gut feeling. They become more rational and the impact of the fluency of the codes gradually becomes smaller.

As we can see, the fluency of the stock codes affects people's economic judgments and decisions-making. Simpler stock codes attract more investors and bring higher returns, particularly in the short term. Although the influence becomes smaller over time, its consequence is likely to be large, especially at the beginning of stock new releases.

Easy-to-read Documents Are More Real and Trustworthy

As another example, imagine you are searching for a book online. You come to an unfamiliar author and find his book description page difficult to read. It has a white background, but its words are written in gray and have distracting shadows. Will you try harder to read about this author or just pass and go on to check others? Perhaps most people will choose the latter.

Here are two versions of the beginning of a book description of mine. Please compare.

Version 1
The world of business is changing.
Productivity and effective leadership are precious commodities.
The right strategies for achieving optimal performance are essential.
Now, with the help of this new book, Fitness Powered Brains, you can improve productivity, performance, and leadership.

Version 2
The world of business is changing.
Productivity and effective leadership are precious commodities.
The right strategies for achieving optimal performance are essential.
Now, with the help of this new book, Fitness Powered Brains, you can improve productivity, performance, and leadership.

In an online shopping scene, psychologists let people read the descriptions of two mobile phones. After reading, people indicated their choices, either to buy the phone or browse the other phones. Half of the subjects

Assumption 4. Being Simple and Salient Is Being Real and Special

were presented a normal font version of the descriptions, like Version 1 above, while the other half were presented with a difficult to read version, like Version 2 above.

Whereas 17% of the subjects viewing Version 1 chose to browse the other phones, 41% of the subjects viewing Version 2 chose to do so. Remember, the contents of the descriptions were exactly the same. A change in fonts brought big differences. Here, the degree of fluency in how information is acquired by the brain—not the information itself—was important.

We often have this kind of experience ourselves. When browsing a slideshow or reading material, if the color or font of the text is somewhat difficult to read, our motivation to continue reading will be greatly affected. We may even have a negative opinion of the document or material and its author. This is also caused by the fluency effect. When information is not clear enough, the degree of fluency is reduced, which causes feelings of insecurity.

In one study, psychologists asked people to read a series of statements about a certain city in a certain country, such as "Lima is in Peru" and "Osorno is in Chile", and judge the accuracy of these statements. These statements were presented in different colors on a white background. As a result, compared to yellow or green, when the statements were presented in dark blue or dark red, people were more likely to judge the statements as true. On a white background, dark blue and red are far easier to read than yellow or green.

Being easy-to-read, with clear font and bold color, is one factor that makes things visually salient. Being salient means catching our attention, triggering vivid images, and leaving us with stronger memories in our mind. Salient information is more fluent.

As a default mindset, we assume that simple and salient information is more real, special, and preferable.

A Picture Is Worth a Thousand Words

Compared to plain words, images are typically better remembered. An influential theory proposed by psychologist Allan Paivio at the University of Western Ontario speculates that, whereas words are primarily represented by verbal codes in the brain, images are more likely to be represented by both verbal and visual/image codes. As the capacity of each mode is limited, this kind of dual-coding reduces the memory load and extends the processing ability, leaving space for more active, deeper encoding.

We read pictures more efficiently, because it would take many words to describe a picture. Thus the saying "a picture is worth a thousand words".

Assumption 4. Being Simple and Salient Is Being Real and Special

In one study, psychologists delivered brain science findings for people to read. It was found that compared to pure findings in text, when the findings were accompanied by illustrative pictures of the brain or bar charts, people evaluated the findings as being more credible. Illustrative pictures of the brain and bar charts are easier to understand and more salient.

In fact, the power of a picture may go beyond our imagination. Using fake pictures, the group of psychologist Elizabeth Loftus at the University of California Irvine successfully planted fake childhood memories in their subjects. In one study, the psychologists artificially synthesized pictures showing their subjects being with the subjects' family members in a high-altitude hot air balloon during childhood, which in fact never happened. After seeing these pictures, subjects were asked to recall this memory. Unbelievably, half of them reported being able to partially or clearly recall the experience.

For example, one participant stated: "*I am sure that this happened in my 6th grade, at school... This was a Saturday. I went with my parents and I am sure my grandma didn't go there. But I'm not sure if there are other people going. I am very sure that my mother took this photo for us on the ground.*"

The psychologists had confirmed with their family members that none of the subjects had gone up in a hot air balloon as a child.

When we are not sure whether something has happened in the past, we usually—and unconsciously—use the fluency of recalling the event as information to judge the possibility of that event. Salient, fluent information, like pictures, is more likely to be perceived as familiar and true, and therefore mistaken as real memory.

Vivid Details Are More Trustworthy

Like pictures, information delivered with vivid details is also salient and persuasive. Sometimes, when someone tries to convince us about something, they usually talk vividly. They deliver their information in great detail, causing us to easily believe in them and in what they say (even while they are lying to us).

Vivid information is more salient to form a mental image in people's mind. It creates a sense of fluency and the latter is taken as true and persuasive. Here, I give you an example.

In a study of simulated law judgments, psychologists designed a case in which a suspected drunk driver caused a traffic accident. At night, the defendant drove home

Assumption 4. Being Simple and Salient Is Being Real and Special

after attending a party. He crossed a stop sign and ran into a garbage truck. The final decision of the judge depended on whether the defendant was driving while drunk.

However, since the driver's blood alcohol concentration was not measured in time, it could only be speculated based on other evidence. Meanwhile, there was evidence the defendant could be relieved of the crime: the garbage truck was gray, so it was not easily identifiable at night.

Psychologists then manipulated the clarity of this evidence to make it beneficial or unfavorable to the defendant. In the suspicion of the accused drunkenness, psychologists let the judge read one of two versions of the description:

A: *"On his way out the door, the defendant staggered against a serving table, knocking a bowl to the floor."*

B: *"On his way out the door, the defendant staggered against a serving table, knocking a bowl of guacamole dip on the white shag carpet."*

In terms of the color of the garbage truck, psychologists also let the judges read one of two versions:

A: *"The owner of the garbage truck admitted under cross-examination that his garbage truck is difficult to see at night because it is grey in color."*

B: *"The owner of the garbage truck admitted under cross-examination that his garbage truck is difficult to see at night because it is grey in color. The owner said his trucks are grey 'because it hides the dirt,' and he said, 'What do you want, I should paint them pink?'"*

As we can see, compared to version A, version B is more detailed and vivid, providing clear mental images.

Consequently, when the judges made the sentences 48 hours later, those who read Version B of the drunkenness text were more likely to evaluate the defendant as guilty. Those who read version B of the garbage truck text more likely evaluated the defendant as not guilty.

In real life, lawyers usually persuade judges through delivering this kind of vivid information and it works quite well. In fact, the greatest contribution of the 20th-century American lawyer Melvin Belli, who is known as the "King of Torts", is the promotion of "demonstrative evidence".

Belli believed that lawyers cannot simply state testimony. Instead, they should present true evidence, using expanded X-rays, complex models, and detailed

Assumption 4. Being Simple and Salient Is Being Real and Special

pictures to demonstrate how the accident occurred and how serious the plaintiff was. In one case, Belli himself used a thick paper to fold out a model of his defendant's lost limb. In that way, the judges could see what happened throughout the trial.

Belli's demonstrative evidence does make it easier for judges to understand the complex cases, but it also greatly enhances the fluency and persuasiveness of the evidence. Perhaps this is why Belli became the "King of Torts".

Be Careful What You Imagine

We have already shown how due to the fact that (1) we assume that fluent memory is more accurate and representative and that fluent information is more real and special, (2) many factors can affect the fluency of memory and information flowing in our mind, and (3) we usually confuse the sources of these fluencies, our attitudes or thoughts toward many things may be flawed.

Psychologists have found that imagining something happening makes people feel that thing is more likely to happen. For instance, psychologists asked subjects to imagine a specific outcome of the next presidential campaign or football game. Later, when asked to evaluate the possibility of various outcomes, the subjects generally thought what they imagined was more likely to occur.

Imagining something happening increases the fluency of that information and creates a sense of familiarity. That information also becomes more accessible during subsequent thinking. This is just like the mere exposure effect, with imagination being a kind of internal exposure.

These phenomena are also consistent with findings in the field of neuroscience. Neuroscientists have discovered that when people read vivid descriptions, the anterior and posterior cortex of the brain responsible for visual images become more active, as if people actually see and experience what is described or imagined. Meanwhile, when people imagine future scenes, their medial prefrontal cortex and medial parietal region become more active. Notably, these brain structures are also responsible for recalling the past. In other words, people think of future things as if those things have actually happened to them.

Interestingly, in real life, we are often unconsciously convinced by this kind of vividness ourselves.

Assumption 4. Being Simple and Salient Is Being Real and Special

Convince Yourself with Imaginations: The Planning Fallacy

In 1976, a team of Israeli educational experts was asked to develop a new curriculum for high school education. At the beginning of this task, each member estimated when they would complete the report and submit it to the Ministry of Education. The estimated time was between 18–30 months.

Although it was made clear that 40% of the teams before them ultimately quit the task halfway through, while others who did complete a report typically spent at least seven years on the report. Nevertheless, the team was sure they could be on schedule, that is, hand in the report within 18–30 months. To their surprise, they completed the report after 8 years of work.

People regularly experience failure, but they still optimistically underestimate the time and cost needed to finish a task. This phenomenon is called "planning fallacy" by decision-making psychologist Daniel Kahneman and Amos Tversky.

Such planning errors are common in various organizational plans, projects, and our daily lives. Research on IT projects shows that on average only about 31.6% of projects were completed as originally planned, 48.6% were postponed or exceeded budget, and 19.8% were canceled midway.

Many people are used to making New Year's resolutions. A survey conducted in the UK found that more than 60% of adults set new year goals and plans. The phenomenon is particularly popular in young adults aged 15–24 years, with up to 80% of them making resolutions. However, only about 9% of people stick to their New Year resolutions for a whole year. In fact, nearly 30% of people give up less than a week into their resolutions. Another study of college students found that 63% of them were unable to complete academic work within their predicted time.

In December 2012, nine months after I started writing a book, I was confident I would finish that book by February 2013. In May 2013, when a friend asked me when I would finish the book, I said August or September. When October arrived, I still felt I needed at least another 2 to 3 months to finish that book.

Why does this happen?

The team of Roger Buehler, a social psychologist at Wilfrid Laurier University in Canada, let people predict how long they would take to complete a series of tasks. However, they had to speak aloud all of their thinking processes in regards to the completion of the task. An average of 71% of people's thinking was about planning and the desired results, 6% was related to memories of a previous successful experience, whereas merely 1% was related to past failures, with another 1% referencing to other people's experience.

That is to say, during the planning process, people mainly focus on the tasks to be completed. They rarely consider the experience of past failures. They constantly assume that the planned content can happen, which makes the planned materials more fluent.

As a result, people mistakenly perceive planned content as more realistic: "The future success just seems so true and close. We can make it."

Look at the Evidence, Objectively

Ken Sheldon, a positive psychologist at the University of Missouri, found that counting one's accomplishments and visually imagining the most successful version of oneself in the future can produce great incentives and improve subsequent performance. This strategy has become an important part of positive psychology.

This chapter has explained how visually imagining one's most successful future self increases the fluency of that image. This method is encouraging and helpful in itself, but its fatal side effect is planning fallacies. We have to remember imagining alone is not enough; we need realistic, doable plans with incremental checkpoints and the ability to look at those plans in a balanced, objective way.

The fluency effect occurs in our life every single day. It is a fundamental feature of the mind because we assume that fluent information is more real and true. This assumption is helpful in guiding our everyday decision-making, but it also may bring biases and flaws to our thoughts.

The most effective strategy for fixing these fluency biases is to find scientific and objective statistics and evidence, and then use them in a correct way. What we need is real, sound, and sufficient evidence.

Furthermore, do not be manipulated by these features of the mind. And avoid solely relying on memory, which is often flawed—although we still should do our best to enhance our memory.

References

Assumption 1. Confirmed Ideas Are Solid and True

Christopher Columbus… Boorstin, D. J. (1985). *The discoverers:[a history of man's search to know world and himself]*. Vintage. pp. 236-244

The confirmation strategy we use… Wason, P. C. (1960). On the failure to eliminate hypotheses in a conceptual task. *Quarterly journal of experimental psychology*, *12*(3), 129-140; Popper, K. (2005). *The logic of scientific discovery*. Routledge; Taleb, N. N. (2007). *The black swan: The impact of the highly improbable*. Random house. pp. 192-193; Nickerson, R. S. (1998). Confirmation bias: A ubiquitous phenomenon in many guises. *Review of general psychology*, *2*(2), 175.

The Hypothetico-Deductive Method… Pence, C. H. (2015). Charles Darwin and Sir John FW Herschel: Nineteenth-Century Science and its Methodology. Available at http://philsci-archive.pitt.edu/8462/1/pence-herschel-eprint.pdf Retrieved 2018-10-20; Taleb, N. N. (2007). *The black swan: The impact of the highly improbable*. Random house

Confirmation biases in psychologists… Hergovich, A., Schott, R., & Burger, C. (2010). Biased evaluation of abstracts depending on topic and conclusion: Further evidence of a confirmation bias within scientific psychology. *Current Psychology*, *29*(3), 188-209; Mahoney, M. J. (1977).

Publication prejudices: An experimental study of confirmatory bias in the peer review system. *Cognitive therapy and research*, *1*(2), 161-175; Armstrong, J. S., & Hubbard, R. (1991). Does the need for agreement among reviewers inhibit the publication controversial findings?. *Behavioral and Brain Sciences*, *14*(1), 136-137.

Confirmation biases in medical doctors... Mendel, R., Traut-Mattausch, E., Jonas, E., Leucht, S., Kane, J. M., Maino, K., ... & Hamann, J. (2011). Confirmation bias: Why psychiatrists stick to wrong preliminary diagnoses. *Psychological Medicine*, *41*(12), 2651-2659.

Confirmation biases in our everyday lives... Darley, J. M., & Gross, P. H. (1983). A hypothesis-confirming bias in labeling effects. *Journal of Personality and Social Psychology*, *44*(1), 20; Snyder, M., & Cantor, N. (1979). Testing hypotheses about other people: The use of historical knowledge. *Journal of Experimental Social Psychology*, *15*(4), 330-342.

Assumption 2. "Handsome Soldiers Are Good at Shooting"

The halo effect... Thorndike, E. L. (1920). A constant error in psychological ratings. *Journal of applied psychology*, *4*(1), 25-29; Epstein, S. (2012). Cognitive-experiential self-theory: An integrative theory of personality. In H. Tennen & J. Suls (Eds.). *Handbook of Psychology, 2ed., Vol.5. Personality Section.* Hoboken, NJ: John Wiley & Sons; Nisbett, R. E., & Wilson, T. D. (1977). The halo effect: evidence for unconscious alteration of judgments. *Journal of personality and social psychology*, *35*(4), 250.

Too high an expectation... Stephen Jay Gould, S.J. (2011) *I have landed: the end of a beginning in natural history.* Belknap Press of Harvard University Press. pp. 102-3.

The illusion of business... Rosenzweig, P. (2014). *The halo effect:... and the eight other business delusions that deceive managers.* Simon and Schuster; Data of Cisco was retrieved from
http://www.wikinvest.com/stock/Cisco_Systems_(CSCO)/Data/Market_Capitalization;
http://investor.cisco.com/stocklookup.cfm?NavSection=StockInfo&historic_Month=12&historic_Day=29&historic_Year=1998;
http://newsroom.cisco.com/dlls/corporate_timeline.pdf   Last accessed 2013-05-27

Risks and benefits under the halo effect... Slovic, P., Finucane, M., Peters, E., & MacGregor, D. (2002). The affect heuristic. In T. Gilovich, D. Griffin, & D. Kahneman, (Eds.), *Intuitive Judgement: Heuristics and Biases.* Cambridge University Press; Finucane, M. L., Alhakami, A., Slovic, P., & Johnson, S. M. (2000). The affect heuristic in judgments of risks and benefits. *Journal of Behavioral Decision Making*, 13, 1-17; Fischhoff B, Slovic P, Lichtenstein S, Read S, Combs B (1978) How Safe is Safe Enough? A Psychometric Study of Attitudes Toward Technological Risks and Benefits. *Policy Sciences* 9:127-152; Verplanken, B. (1989). Beliefs, attitudes, and intentions toward nuclear energy before and after Chernobyl in a longitudinal within-subjects design. *Environment and Behavior*, *21*(4), 371-392; Visschers, V. H., & Siegrist, M. (2013). How a nuclear power plant accident influences acceptance of nuclear power: Results of a longitudinal study before and after the Fukushima disaster. *Risk Analysis: An International Journal*, *33*(2), 333-347; Kaustia, M., Laukkanen, H., & Puttonen, V. (2009). Should good stocks have high prices or high returns?. *Financial Analysts Journal*, *65*(3), 55-62.

How to overcome the halo effect… Cooper, W.H. (1981).Ubiquitous halo. *Psychological Bulletin*, 90, 218-244; Borman, W. C. (1975). Effects of instructions to avoid halo error on reliability and validity of performance evaluation ratings. *Journal of Applied Psychology*, 60, 556-560.

Assumption 3. Fluent Memories Are More Compelling and Trustable

"If I cannot recall it"… Winkielman, P., Schwarz, N. & Belli, R. F. (1998). The role of ease of retrieval and attribution in memory judgments: Judging your memory as worse despite recalling more events. *Psychological Science*, 9,124-126; Schwarz, N., Bless, H., Strack, F., Klumpp, G., Rittenauer-Schatka, H., & Simons, A. (1991). Ease of retrieval as information: Another look at the availability heuristic. *Journal of Personality and Social Psychology*, 61, 195-202; Schwarz, N., Sanna, L.J., Skurnik, I., & Yoon, C. (2007). Metacognitive experiences and the intricacies of setting people straight:

Implications for debiasing and public information campaigns. *Advances in Experimental Social Psychology* 39: 127-161.

Sampling traps… Wilson, T. D., Hodges, S. D., & LaFleur, S. J. (1995). Effects of introspecting about reasons: Inferring attitudes from accessible thoughts. *Journal of Personality and Social Psychology*, 69, 16–28.

What happens after a man view an ad 20 times… Thomas Smith quoted in Alan G. Sawyer (1982),"The Effects of Repetition and Levels of Processing on Learning and Attitudes", in NA - *Advances in Consumer Research* Volume 09, eds. Andrew Mitchell, Ann Abor, MI: Association for Consumer Research, pp. 439-443.

The mere exposure effect… Zajonc, R. B. (1968). Attitudinal effects of mere exposure. *Journal of personality and social psychology*, 9(2p2), 1; Zajonc, R. B. (2001). Mere exposure: A gateway to the subliminal. *Current directions in psychological science*, 10(6), 224-228; Smith GH & Engel R, 1968, Influence of a Female Model on Perceived Characteristics of an Automobile, *Proceedings from the 76th APA Annual Convention*, 681-682.

Human kindness, or thinking bias… Moreland, R. L., & Beach, S. R. (1992). Exposure effects in the classroom: The development of affinity among students. *Journal of Experimental Social Psychology*, 28, 255-276; Verrier, D. (2012). Evidence for the influence of the mere-exposure effect on voting in the Eurovision Song Contest. *Judgement and Decision Making*, 7(5), 639-643.

Be careful what you expose yourself to... Villani, S. (2001). Impact of media on children and adolescents: A 10-year review of the research. *Journal of the American Academy of Child and Adolescent Psychiatry*, 40(4), 392-401; Grube, J.W. & L.Wallack (1994) Television beer advertising and drinking knowledge, beliefs, and intentions among schoolchildren. *American Journal of Public Health*, 84(2):254-259; Pierce JP, Choi WS, Gilpin EA, Farkas AJ, Berry CC. 1998 Tobacco industry promotion of cigarettes and adolescent smoking. *JAMA*; 279: 511-515; Wood, W., Wong, F., & Chachere, J. G. (1991). Effects of media violence on viewers' aggression in unconstrained social interaction. *Psychological Bulletin*, 109, 371-83; Paik, H., & Comstock, G. (1994). The effects of television violence on antisocial behavior: A meta-analysis. *Communication Research*, 21, 516-546.

Assumption 4. Being Simple and Salient Is Being More Real and Special

"Fluent" stocks make more money... Alter, A. L. & Oppenheimer, D. M. (2006). Predicting short-term stock fluctuations by using processing fluency. *Proceedings of the National Academy of Science*, 103, 9369-9372.

Easy-to-read documents are more real... Novemsky, N., Dhar, R., Schwarz, N., & Simonson, I. (2007). Preference fluency in choice. *Journal of Marketing Research*, 44, 347-356; Reber,

References

R., & Schwarz, N. (1999). Effects of perceptual fluency on judgments of truth. *Consciousness and Cognition*, 8, 338-342.

A picture is worth a thousand words... Paivio, A. (2013). *Imagery and verbal processes*. Psychology Press; Frenda, S. F., Nichols, R. M., & Loftus, E. F. (2011). Current Issues and Advances in Misinformation Research. *Current Directions in Psychological Science*, 20, 20-3; Loftus, E. F. (2004). Memories of things unseen. *Current Directions in Psychological Science*, 13, 145-147; Wade, K. A., Garry, M., Read, J. D., & Lindsay, D. S. (2002). A picture is worth a thousand lies: Using false photographs to create false childhood memories. *Psychonomic Bulletin & Review*, *9*(3), 597-603.

Vivid details are more trustable... Reyes, R. M., Thompson, W. C., & Bower, G. H. (1980). Judgmental biases resulting from differing availabilities of arguments. *Journal of Personality and Social Psychology*, *39*(1), 2; Page, Joseph A., "Roscoe Pound, Melvin Belli, and the Personal-Injury Bar: The Tale of an Odd Coupling" (2009). *Georgetown Law Faculty Publications and Other Works*. Paper 378.

Be careful what you imagine... Koehler, D. J. (1991), Explanation, imagination, and confidence in judgment. *Psychological Bulletin*, 110, 499-519; Schacter DL, Guerin SA, St Jacques PL. 2011 Memory distortion: an adaptive perspective. *Trends Cogn Sci*. 15(10):467-74.

Convince yourself with your imaginations... Kahneman, D., & Tversky, A. (1979). Intuitive prediction: Biases and corrective procedures. *TIMS Studies in Management Science*, 12, 313-327; Kahneman, D., & Egan, P. (2011). *Thinking, fast and slow*(Vol. 1). New York: Farrar, Straus and Giroux; The Standish Group (2009). *CHAOS summary 2009*. Boston, MA: Standish Group International Inc.; New year resolutions, retrieved http://www.prnewswire.co.uk/news-releases/slim-chance-of-resolution-success-says-mcvities-go-ahead-survey-156804105.html Last accessed 2013-09-24; Buehler, R., Griffin, D. and Ross, M. (1994). Exploring the "planning fallacy": Why people underestimate their task completion times. *Journal of Personality and Social Psychology*, 67: 366-381.

Look at the evidence... Sheldon, K. M., & Lyubomirsky, S. (2006). How to increase and sustain positive emotion: The effects of expressing gratitude and visualizing best possible selves. *Journal of Positive Psychology*, 1, 73-82.

Index

Allan Paivio, 68

Alzheimer, 18, 20, 21

Amerigo Vespucci, 7

Amos Tversky, 75

Chernobyl, 38, 41, 82

Christopher Columbus, 3, 5, 7, 79

Daniel Kahneman, 75

Daniel M. Oppenheimer, 63

Edward Lee Thorndike, 28

European Song Contest, 60, 61

George Bernard Shaw, 43

George E. Nunn, 4

Hypothetico-Deductive Method, 13, 14, 15, 79

John Chambers, 34, 35

John Henslow, 33

John Herschel, 13, 32

Karl Popper, 10, 11, 26

Ken Sheldon, 77

King of Torts, 72, 73

Melvin Belli, 72, 85

Nassim Nicholas Taleb, 3

Norbert Schwarz, 48

Paul Slovic, 38

Peter C. Wason, 11

Princeton University, 63

Robert B. Zajonc, 54

Roger Buehler, 76

Strategic Memory, 3, 50

The Black Swan, 3

The Impact of the Highly Improbable, 3

The Natural History of Learning and Forgetting, 3, 51

The Travels of Marco Polo, 3

University of Michigan, 48

University of Missouri, 77

University of Oregon, 38

University of Western Ontario, 68

Wilfrid Laurier University, 76

About the Author

Dr. Chong Chen is a neuroscientist and an assistant professor of psychiatry. He possesses a Ph.D. in Medicine and has authored two book series called *The Anchor of Our Purest Thoughts* and *Your Baby's Developing Brain*.

As far as the future goes, Chong hopes that he will be able to translate scientific findings into ways that will allow regular people to live better lives. And through his books, he hopes that he can reach a much wider audience.

You can contact Chong and follow what he is writing about at: https://brainandlife.net.

www.ingramcontent.com/pod-product-compliance
Lightning Source LLC
Chambersburg PA
CBHW031412040426
42444CB00005B/533